PRESENTED TO:

Dylan Felty

FROM:

First Christian Church

DATE:

May 21, 2023

WHAT PEOPLE ARE SAYING ABOUT
CATCHING JESUS

It keeps the interest of my players because it ties examples of baseball to show or make a point in the teachings of the word. It makes learning about Jesus fun and exciting because they can relate to it so well. It catches your interest and keeps it! Wonderful book!
- Brett Brinson, Aces 18U Elite coach

As a mom of four kids, I love how this book lays out real life scenarios and makes a connection back to the bible. It's easy to read and understand which is so important for children. It is also to the point which helps with time in our busy lives.
- Ashlee Little, baseball mom

This book is a homerun! Everything relates back to the word of the Lord. Definitely a book for baseball lovers to read and learn from.
- Jesse Boone, 11, baseball player

Catching Jesus

Daily Devotions with a Baseball Theme

AMY MCNEILL

Catching Jesus by Amy McNeill
Copyright © 2016 by Amy McNeill
All rights reserved.

Scripture content from The New Living Translation (NLT) Copyright © 2005 Used by permission of Tyndale House Publishers, Inc. All rights reserved.
Scripture content from the New International Version (NIV) ©1984, 2011 Used by permission of Zondervan. All rights reserved.
Scripture content from the New International Reader's Version (NIRV) ©1996 Used by permission of International Bible Society. All rights reserved.

Title page image credit: 123rf.com/kreinick
Interior Images: stock, used by permission
Book Design/Publishing Assistant:
The Author's Mentor, www.theauthorsmentor.com
Author email: catchingjesus@gmail.com
Author Website: www.facebook.com/catchingjesus

ISBN-13: 978-1537133010
ISBN-10: 1537133012

PUBLISHED IN THE UNITED STATES OF AMERICA

...from the Author

My son played travel baseball, which sometimes had us absent from church on Sunday mornings. I began writing these devotions and spending five minutes with the boys before the game. This quickly became my favorite part of the tournament and proved that you can worship anywhere.

I love teaching young people about the eternal love of Jesus Christ. I have always enjoyed sports and creative writing. Having the opportunity to combine all three has been a true blessing. The word of God can be applied to baseball and all areas of your life. I pray that you will learn and grow in your faith as you read this book.

Amy McNeill lives in Albemarle, NC, with her husband Gary and three children, Kolbie, Korbin, and Kinslie.

The Lineup

The Baseball

DID YOU KNOW EVERY OFFICIAL MAJOR LEAGUE BASEBALL IS MADE PRECISELY WITH CERTAIN REQUIREMENTS?

The core center is a 4 1/8 inch round pill made of cork and rubber. Layered around the pill is a four-ply white yarn, followed by a three-ply gray yarn, and lastly a white cotton yarn. Each layer is tightly wrapped which brings the unfinished baseball to slightly less than 9 inches. The cover of the baseball is number one grade cowhide from Midwest Holstein cattle because they produce the best hides in the US. The baseball is then hand-stitched together with precisely 108 stitches of red thread.

Why is it important to make each baseball the exact same? Yes, for consistency. All the careful measures and precise details put in to making a baseball doesn't begin to compare to all the details God focused on when making you.

Lift your arm in front of you, bend your elbow, rotate your wrist and wiggle your fingers. Seems simple until you think about how many muscles and bones had to coordinate together to perform those tasks. Think about when you run and your whole body is moving together without any complications. Your body is also capable of doing some things on its own, such as blinking and breathing. Whether the movements are voluntary or involuntary, it would not work the same if one measurement was wrong or one piece was missing.

Now, think about inside your body. Wow – talk about complicated! Your brain, spinal cord, heart, lungs, liver, kidneys, intestines and other organs all work together every day. If one organ doesn't do its job, then other problems arise. Down to the very smallest cell in your body, God designed you. He orchestrated how each section of your body functions individually to make the whole creation synchronized. God is precise in every detail and He is the master of creation.

So, when you look at how precisely made a baseball is, take a minute to thank God for being so specific in making every detail of your body.

> *Thank you for making me*
> *so wonderfully complex! Your*
> *workmanship is marvelous –*
> *how well I know it.*
> Psalm 139:14 NLT

GOING DEEP ...
Do you feel special? Why or why not?

_____

_____

_____

Anticipation

ANTICIPATION IS THE EXPECTATION OR HOPE OF SOMETHING BEFORE IT HAPPENS.

If you shake up a soda and then open it, what do you expect will happen? If you study really hard for a test, what do you expect will happen? If you jump out of an airplane, what do you expect will happen?

You are playing third base and you see the batter square up. What do you anticipate? You are up to bat waiting for the next pitch. What are you hoping for? You are an outfielder and you hear the crack of the bat. What do you do?

Baseball is a game of anticipation. You are constantly thinking about what could happen next and what your action will be. The greatest players in baseball

Amy McNeill

are those that are masters of anticipation. The top batters are mentally prepared to predict where the next pitch will be thrown and how they will conquer it. What do Barry Bonds, Albert Pujols, Mike Piazza, and Brian Giles have in common? They were all struck out by softball player Jennie Finch! Why do you think that is? The reason is because they were unable to anticipate the speed and motion of the softball since it is so different than that of the baseball they are used to.

In the book of Psalms, there is a Hebrew word – *qadam*. Translated to English, the word means "to come meet" or "to anticipate a meeting". The word does not mean wait until tomorrow or when I get a chance. It means come quickly, do not hesitate. In baseball we want to use *qadam*, without pausing in our actions. But, more important than baseball, God desires us to anticipate Him. He wants us to come quickly to Him daily. Because Jesus died on the cross for us, we can anticipate seeing

6

Him one day when we spend eternity in Heaven. We should live our lives anticipating the outcome of our decisions so we can make wise choices. God loves you and he is proud of you on and off the baseball field. Always try to do your best, anticipate your next step and come quickly.

Call to me and I will answer you and tell you great and unsearchable things you do not know.
Jeremiah 33:3 NIV

GOING DEEP ...
Write of a time you when you were really looking forward to something. Was it what you expected? How did you feel?

_____

_____

_____

A Perfect Game

WHAT IS A PERFECT GAME?

According to the Major League Baseball (MLB), a perfect game is when no batter on the opposing team safely reaches first base throughout a completed game. That means no walks, no infield errors, no missed diving catches by an outfielder, no homeruns. That is 27 batters and 27 outs – no exceptions, no mistakes, no second chances.

How difficult is this? The first perfect game recorded in the MLB was in 1880. Since then, there have only been 21 perfect games! In fact, more people have been to the moon (24 people) than have pitched a perfect game. That's impressive!

As you can imagine, it would take a lot of focus to maintain this perfect effort for nine complete innings. Can you imagine being perfect all the time? It is actually impossible for us, but there is one man who is perfect – Jesus Christ. Jesus walked on this Earth for 33 years and was perfect the entire time! No sin, no mistakes, no wrongs. You may think, "Things were different then, he didn't have my life". You're right. It is not exactly the same, but Jesus did live a life that had some similarities. He was born as a baby to a non-wealthy family. He lived with his parents and siblings. When Jesus got older he helped his father as a carpenter. Jesus helped and loved others even when it wasn't accepted by others. He and His disciples taught people lessons about why they should trust in God. The ultimate lesson was taught by Jesus when He was willingly nailed to the cross and took our sin as His own. As He suffered, bled and died for us, He was the perfect example of love. End of the story?

Absolutely not! Jesus rose from the grave and lives in Heaven. He is waiting for us there.

Just like it is highly unlikely that you will ever participate in a perfect MLB game, God knows you cannot live a life as perfect as Jesus. He does not expect you to be flawless. He made you with your own independent mind and the ability to make your own choices. It pleases Him greatly when you choose to be His follower, but that's a decision you must make on your own. You can choose to live your life pleasing to Him by following His word and studying the perfect game played by Jesus.

Don't copy the behavior and customs of this world, but let God transform you into a new person by changing the way you think. Then you will learn to know God's will for you, which is good and pleasing and perfect.
Romans 12:2 NLT

11

GOING DEEP ...
Do you feel it was difficult for Jesus to live on Earth? Why?

Homerun

THE OFFICIAL DEFINITION OF A HOMERUN IS A HIT IN WHICH THE BATTER SCORES BY CIRCLING ALL THE BASES AND REACHING HOME PLATE IN ONE PLAY.

The top three homerun records are held by Barry Bonds (762), Hank Aaron (755) and Babe Ruth (714). The longest distance homerun record is held by Mickey Mantle (660 feet). The longest streak of 30 or more homeruns in a season for thirteen straight seasons is held by both Barry Bonds and Alex Rodriquez.

So, a homerun doesn't just happen the very first time you pick up a bat, right? You have to learn how to hold your bat, where to put your feet, when to bend your knees and flex your arms, how to keep your eye on the ball, and above all, know when to swing. Simple, right? Not at all ... this takes practice, practice, and more practice. Let's imagine this is your moment to hit your first homerun. You hear the crack of the bat as it meets perfectly with the rotating ball. For a moment, everything is in slow motion as the crowd jumps to their feet. It's going, it's going, and it's gone! You did it!

What an amazing feeling! You run to first base pumping your fist in the air. You circle second base and give the friendly short stop a high five. As you round third, you see your mom taking a picture. Then, you jog to home plate as all of your teammates anxiously await you. The fans are clapping and cheering your name.

Now, you may have read that and thought, "Well, that will never happen to me. I am just happy when I can get a base hit." Let me tell you some great news! Jesus has already hit a homerun for you, but he needs you to run the bases. At first base, you admit you are a sinner. If you need help, your base coach is right there to give you advice. When you get to second base, you have to believe with all your heart, mind, and soul that Jesus died for you and He lives again. While running to third base, you see your base coach waiting to listen. Confess to him that you have been saved- Jesus is your Lord and Savior. Then, your mom will probably still want to take a picture. For the rest of your life on Earth, you will run home. One day, when you reach home plate, all the angels in Heaven will be cheering for you. Your name will be in Heaven's Hall of Fame. Are you willing to run the bases for Him?

Therefore, since we are surrounded by such a huge crowd of witnesses to the life of faith, let us strip off every weight that slows us down, especially the sin that so easily trips us up. And let us run with endurance the race God has set before us.
Hebrews 12:1 NLT

GOING DEEP ...

Have you already accepted Jesus? If yes, write the details of your amazing experience. If not, write down some questions you want to ask someone.

Curveball

A CURVEBALL IS A TYPE OF PITCH WITH A CERTAIN HANDGRIP AND MOVEMENT THAT CAUSES THE BALL TO HAVE A FORWARD SPIN; THUS CAUSING IT TO MOVE UNEXPECTEDLY.

You are in the batter's box ready for the pitch. You are prepared – you were hitting great earlier in the batting cage. Your team and fans are cheering you on for a big hit. You see the windup. The ball is revealed and your eyes are focused. You grip your bat a little tighter. The ball gets closer. You swing with all your might. You hear, "Strike one!" Wait a minute – that ball moved! You didn't know that curve ball was coming! That is not fair!

Has this ever happened to you? How about off the baseball field? Have you ever had a pop quiz? How about a surprise Ipod inspection by your parents? Maybe you have dealt with something worse like a divorce or a death in your family? These are some curve balls in life - things that are unexpected and sometimes just not fair!

There was a man in the Bible named Job. Job had more curveballs thrown at him than you could imagine. All the animals he owned were stolen. He became sick with painful sores on his body. His children all died. People mocked him because of the struggles he had. Life definitely was not fair for Job. But the Bible says that Job was thankful to God. You're kidding me, right? He was happy about all those bad things? No. Job understood the things he lost were given to him by God. So, if God so chooses to take them away, He is to be praised for knowing best. Job took his feelings and questions to God but never wavered his faith in the Lord. Many curveballs will make you sad, some even make you angry but you can take all of your emotions to the Lord. Tell Him how you feel and trust that He will show you the way. Remember, God has a plan for your life. There will be curveballs, but He will never leave you. So, when life or baseball doesn't seem fair, take a deep breath and remember God is in control. Show your faith in Him by your actions and positive influence on others.

Trust in the Lord with all your heart; do not depend on your own understanding.
Proverbs 3:5 NLT

GOING DEEP ...

What is the worst curveball in life you have had to deal with? How did you cope with your feelings?

_____

_____

_____

Rulebook

WHY DO WE HAVE RULES IN BASEBALL?

Have you ever played Monopoly with someone that plays with different rules than you? It not only makes it confusing, but it is not fair for either of you. The same is true with baseball. If we didn't all follow the same rules, the game would be unorganized and difficult to play.

Generally the MLB uses the same rules you do on your baseball team. 3 strikes, 4 balls, 3 outs … But, did you know there are some unique rules still in the MLB rulebook today?

→ A pitcher is not allowed to throw a spit ball or in any way wet the ball before pitching.

→ Players of opposing teams are not allowed to "hang out" with each other while in uniform.

→ If a fielder uses his hat to catch or stop a ball, the runner is awarded three bases.

Sometimes rules can seem out of date, but most of the time rules are made to control, protect, or make something better.

The most famous and well used set of rules is The Ten Commandments:

1. Do not worship anyone else
2. Do not make idols
3. Honor God's name
4. Keep the Sabbath day holy
5. Honor your father and mother
6. Do not murder
7. Do not cheat
8. Do not steal
9. Do not tell lies about others
10. Do not wish for someone else's possessions

God gave the rules to Moses to share with the people that left Egypt. God would be using this group of people to start a new nation. He wanted them to know how to worship Him only and how they should treat each other. Now, He did not say, "here are some suggestions, use them if you feel like it." No. These are commandments. He commanded and required these rules to be followed. The beauty of God's word is that it does not become outdated. The rules were important for society then, and they are still important for. us today. Can you imagine the chaos we would live in without these commandments? God loves us enough to provide us with a rulebook. He has given us guidance on what is right and what is wrong. Be thankful for the fairness rules provide in baseball and in life.

Remember, it is sin to know what you ought to do and then not do it.
James 4:17 NLT

GOING DEEP ...

Do you think it is fair to receive punishment when you break the rules? Why or why not?

Base Running

WHO IS THE FASTEST RUNNER ON YOUR TEAM?

Rickey Henderson holds the record for the most stolen bases in an MLB career with 1,406. The fastest recorded time to circle the bases was 13.3 seconds, set by Evar Swanson in 1932.

Base running is a skill that requires agility, speed, and mental quickness. When you are on base and your coach gives you the sign to steal, do you jog over to second base while humming your favorite tune? No! You run full speed while all your attention is focused on your target. You fully intend to get there before the ball does. Do you think Rickey Henderson could have stolen all those bases had he not been focused on doing his best? Are you going to be safe every time you steal? No, but you always give it your all.

On several occasions in the Bible, we are given instructions to try to do our best. The disciple Luke asks "If you are not going to try to finish the race, why even bother starting?" The apostle Paul writes, "In everything you do, do it with all your heart for God, not to impress others." God wants us to run each area of our life just like we are trying to score at home plate. When you know you have a big Math test coming up, God expects you to prepare for it. When your parents go to work, God expects them to use the abilities He has given them. When a friend is having a difficult time, God expects you to help them. When you are assigned chores to do at home, God expects you to obey without complaining. Do you think God cares about you playing baseball? Absolutely! He adores you. But, here's the key, He doesn't care if you win or lose. He doesn't care what your batting average is. He doesn't care if you made the winning catch. He only cares that you are trying your best and showing good character.

So, whether you are playing baseball, sitting in class, or relaxing at home, God is watching you run the race. He is your biggest fan, and one day, He will be standing at the finish line with your prize. Your reward in Heaven will be far greater than any MLB record!

Don't you realize that in a race everyone runs, but only one person get the prize? So run to win!
1 Corinthians 9:24 NLT

GOING DEEP …
Write the details of a time when you gave it your all. How did you feel physically and emotionally?

_____

_____

_____

_____

_____

_____

_____

_____

_____

_____

_____

_____

_____

_____

_____

Choices

THE 1919 WORLD SERIES FEATURED THE CHICAGO WHITE SOX AGAINST THE CINCINNATI REDS.

Shortly after the series, Joe Jackson, centerfielder for the White Sox, and seven other players were accused of throwing the series for a payoff of $5,000 per player. This was more than double their normal salary. The players appeared in court and were permanently banned from the MLB. The famous line of disappointment from a newspaper headline was

"Say it ain't so Joe." Unfortunately, whether it was true or not, the damage had already been done.

You have choices every time you play baseball. Outfielders judge if they should run up or stay back. Infielders decide to cover the base or close the gap. Pitchers decide which pitch to throw. Batters decide if they should swing or take the first pitch. Many choices take place in a single game of baseball.

In your life you also have choices every day. What to wear? What to eat? Study for a test? Do your homework? Be nice to your sister? Clean your room? Read your Bible?

As you get older you will have more choices. Should I be friends with this person? Do I need to say something to the bully in my class? What if I disobey my parents? Have I disrespected my teacher? Should I use ugly language? Are my actions inappropriate?

Here's the truth: You can choose your choices, but you can't choose your consequences. Every choice has a reaction. Some are good and some are bad.

In the Bible, Adam and Eve made a bad choice. They disobeyed God's orders and had to be punished. They were banished from the beautiful Garden of Eden. Adam and Eve were ashamed and remorseful, but were unable to reverse the choice they made.

Joe Jackson, one of baseball's great players never had the chance to finish his baseball career and is not eligible for the Hall of Fame, all over one choice. He made his choice, but certainly didn't predict the consequences.

While you are on the field, at school, or at home, always try to make the best choice. Take a minute to think about the situation and ask for help if you need it. Don't ever sacrifice what you know is right. Be thankful God chooses to love you!

A childish person believes anything. But a wise person thinks about how he lives.
Proverbs 14:15 NIRV

GOING DEEP ...

List a time when you made the right choice and a time when you made the wrong choice. What was the difference? What were the consequences?

Slump

A "HITTING SLUMP" IS A STREAK OF NO HITS.

It only happens to the worst players, right? No! Check this out:

> Mickey Mantle 0-20 (1960)
> Willie Mays 0-24 (1965)
> Reggie Jackson 0-35 (1983)
> Derek Jeter 0-32 (2004)

The top three reasons that cause a slump are:
1. Over thinking
2. Doubting your ability
3. Pressure on yourself

All three of the above reasons are mental. This means there is nothing wrong with you, and it can change today. You can't change the past, but today may be the start of a hitting streak for you.

So, in life, what if you are in a slump? What if you have never read a Bible? What if you haven't prayed in a few weeks? Have you sinned by lying to your parents? What if you have gossiped? How do you correct the issues you are struggling with?

In the Bible, Paul tells us that when our minds are clogged up with non-righteous thoughts, we are separated from God. This separation can cause us to lose the ability to have good judgment, doubt ourselves, and lose confidence. The longer we are apart from God, the further we fall into a slump.

Just like a hitting slump, a spiritual slump you are experiencing needs to be left in the past. You can only change today. Clear your mind of distractions, ask God for forgiveness, and pray for renewed passion. God will meet you exactly where you are. He doesn't ask you to back up and do something over. He doesn't ask you to accomplish some big task. If you turn to Him, He will accept you just the way you are. He will come to you with His arms wide open and pull you out of that slump. He loves you and wants to be close to you today.

> *Come close to God and He will come close to you.*
> James 4:8 NLT

GOING DEEP ...
What kind of slump are you in? What are the steps you need to take to do better?

_____

_____

_____

_____

_____

Catching Jesus

Coach

GROWING UP, TERRY FRANCONA ALWAYS DREAMED OF PLAYING IN THE MLB.

He played baseball at the University of Arizona, and was named college player of the year in 1980. He made his way through the minor leagues and was thrilled to play his first major league game with the Montreal Expos on August 19th, 1981. Proving himself as an asset, he led the league with his batting average. After a few seasons, a strange incident changed his plans. Terry hit the ball down the first base line. The pitcher scooped the ball and went to tag Terry. Trying to avoid the tag, Terry ducked and heard his left knee pop. He was only 25 years old and his promising career was now over due to an injury.

Disappointed, but determined to find a way to continue in the sport he loved, Terry found a coaching position. His passion for the game, paired with his experience, let Terry know that this was exactly what God had planned. Terry coached the Boston Red Sox to World Series titles in 2004 and 2007. Terry's motto: "Turn challenges into opportunities."

Think of the qualities of a good coach. Have you ever seen them get frustrated? Have you ever seen them get excited? Why do you think they have this range of emotions? The reason is because they believe in you and they desire for you to succeed. They know you can do it. They want to help you be better – not just in baseball, but in life as well. They spend their time because they are invested in you. Take the advice from your coach and try to improve in the areas that will make you better.

When Jesus was on Earth, He coached a team of disciples. Each had their own strengths and weaknesses, but

Jesus taught them how to come together for His mission. Did He have challenges? Yes! Some of the disciples argued with each other. Some of them fought for Jesus' attention. Some of them betrayed Jesus. Being the coach of this team was not easy, but Jesus gave the disciples the opportunities to witness to other people and share the love of God. Guess what? He has invited you to be on His team as well! He believes in you more than you will ever know, and He wants you to share that with your friends! Anytime you want to know more about being on Jesus' team, read your Bible or ask someone that lives the example of God's love. When you are on Jesus' team it becomes easier to turn challenges into opportunities.

I am the Lord your God. I take hold of your right hand. I say to you "Do not be afraid. I will help you."
Isaiah 41:13 NIRV

GOING DEEP ...

Can you think of anyone in your life that has turned a challenge into an opportunity? What lesson can you learn from them?

Foul Ball

A FOUL BALL IS ONE THAT IS HIT OUTSIDE THE FIRST BASELINE OR THIRD BASELINE.

While playing for the St. Louis Cardinals, Enos Slaughter once fouled off 26 balls during one at bat.

In 1957, Philadelphia outfielder Richie Ashburn fouled off 14 pitches. One of the foul balls hit a woman in the stands breaking her nose. While she was being carried out of the stadium, Ashburn fouled another pitch that hit the same woman a second time!

Have you ever seen someone up to bat that fouls off a ball? Then a second ball? Followed by a third, a fourth, a fifth? Have you ever heard the umpire say, "That's it! I can't handle this anymore?" No. You continue to battle

with unlimited foul chances. Have you
heard the coaches say, "Oh, you're
terrible, this stinks, stop fouling the
ball?" No. They say, "Good try", "Way
to get a piece of it", "Hang in there",
"Don't give up", "You'll get this next
one." Well, the truth is, sometimes you
get it and sometimes you don't. But, if
you messed up the first time, you can
have a chance to correct it on the next
try.

This is the way God is with us. In
life, our foul balls are called sins. We
are human – we will all sin and we will
make mistakes. Even all the great
people in the Bible have sinned ...
Adam, David, Abraham, Moses. Our
God has unlimited love and forgiveness
for us, but remember, He despises sin!
He wants you to try your best to hit all
the balls fair. But, when you
occasionally foul it off, He will be there
to give you a second, third, and fourth
chance. He will be the one encouraging
you to try it again and get it right. God
expects us to repent for our sins. The

definition of repent is to turn away. This means we leave the mistake behind, try our best to never repeat that mistake, and ask God to forgive us. Once we have done that, it is wiped away; we don't have to carry that load with us any longer. When we are forgiven God smiles and says, "Ok, get back in the batter's box. It's your turn to get a hit."

But God is faithful and fair. If we admit that we have sinned, He will forgive us our sins. He will forgive every wrong thing we have done.
He will make us pure.
1 John 1:9 NIRV

GOING DEEP ...
Have you ever felt hopeless? What inspired you to keep trying?

_____

_____

_____

Confidence

CONFIDENCE IS THE FEELING OR BELIEF THAT YOU CAN FIRMLY TRUST SOMETHING OR SOMEONE.

"It's hard to beat a person who never gives up."

- Babe Ruth

"A person always doing his best becomes a natural leader by example."

- Joe DiMaggio

"It isn't hard to be good from time to time. What is tough is being good every day."

- Willie Mays

"You have to keep running. I always believed I was going to be safe."

- Rickey Henderson

Amy McNeill

    What is your position on the baseball
field? Think about the confidence you
need to play in that spot. A pitcher
needs to know they can throw strikes. A
catcher is daring a base runner to steal
so he can have the opportunity to throw
him out. An infielder is ready to turn the
double play. An outfielder is begging for
a fly ball. When you step in the batter's
box, you are confident you are going to
hit the ball.
    There   are   many   examples   of
confidence in the Bible. One of the best
is about a young shepherd boy named
David. He was not the expected choice
to battle a 9 foot tall giant from the
Philistine army, but David was confident
that God would provide. Goliath the
giant had a huge physical advantage and
was far more equipped with weapons.
David was determined to face the giant
with his slingshot and stones. This is
how David had fought off the wild
animals that would try to attack his
sheep. He was skilled with the weapon

of his choice, but greater than that, was his unwavering faith in the Lord. Everyone expected David to be scared but through his strength in God, he was able to overcome his fears and strike down Goliath.

Do you think David said, "Umm, maybe I can do it?" Or, "I'll give it a try and see what happens?" No! Without his faith, David would have been killed by Goliath. God delivered David from harm. Believe in God's protection and have faith in all that you do. Know that you are who God wants you to be and every time you step on that field, have confidence because you follow Him.

This is my command - be strong and courageous! Do not be afraid or discouraged. For the Lord your God is with you wherever you go.
Joshua 1:9 NLT

GOING DEEP ...
List a time when you were scared but had to find courage.

Differences

UNIQUE, SPECIAL, DISTINCT

In 1951, St Louis Browns' player Eddie Gaedel made history by being the shortest MLB player ever. He was 3'7". The tallest MLB player to date is the 6'11" Kansas City Royals relief pitcher, Jon Rauch. The oldest person to play MLB was 59 year old Satchel Paige for the Cleveland Indians, and the youngest was a 15 year old pitcher named Joe Nuxhall for the Cincinnati Reds.

Think about your friends or your team mates. Do you look alike? Are you the same height? Are you the same weight? Do you have the same strengths or weaknesses?

God made each of us different. We were not placed in a machine and passed down an assembly line. No one asked our parents for their preferences. God personally and lovingly selected your body, your eye color, your hair color, and the placement of every freckle. He knew exactly when you would be born. He knows what you are doing at this moment, and He knows what you will look like when you are 70. This means you are special! There is no one else like you! You are one of a kind! If He took the time to create every little detail about you, then how could it be wrong? You are completely and exactly the way He wants you to be. That does not mean you have no responsibility. God wants you to improve yourself. He wants you to be the best you can be. The great news is... He equips you with the ability to be better. He provides you with everything you need.

So, delight in your differences knowing you were chosen by God. Try to be a better ball player, a better student, a better son, a better brother and a better friend. But most of all, remember the One that allows you to be more than you are. God created you to be different and being different is good.

> *For we are God's masterpiece. He has created us anew in Christ Jesus, so we can do the good things He planned for us long ago.*
> *Ephesians 2:10 NLT*

GOING DEEP ...
Name some physical features that make you unique. Do you like your special traits?

_____

_____

_____

_____

_____

_____

Anger

ANGER IS DEFINED AS A STRONG FEELING OF ANNOYANCE, DISPLEASURE, OR HOSTILITY.

Do you ever see anyone angry in baseball? I bet sometimes you see your coach get angry. Here are MLB examples of anger going too far.

In 1956, Baltimore Orioles manager Paul Richards was ejected 12 times in one season.

Atlanta Braves manager Bobby Cox holds the all-time record for career game ejections with 161.

In 2000, the Chicago White Sox and the Detroit Tigers had a fight causing 25 players and coaches to be ejected in one game.

Anger in baseball or in life comes from a deep passion for something.

Have you ever experienced anger? Do you think Jesus was ever angry?

In the book of Matthew we are told of a sacred place called the temple. People from all around would travel miles by foot to go to the temple. It was a holy place that was designed for people to worship, confess their sin and bring offerings. This was a very special place and it deserved respect.

Unfortunately, people allowed things to happen in the temple that should not have happened. Picture a yard sale in your church sanctuary – people selling jewelry and clothing, some trading goats and sheep, passing money back and forth in a place that is supposed to be honored. This was definitely wrong! Matthew tells us that Jesus walked in the temple and was angry! He turned over the tables and grabbed a whip made of cord. He was extremely disappointed in what he found. Do you think Jesus' reaction was justified?

Think about your life. Are there times that Jesus would walk in on your situation and turn over tables? Do you think He would be angry at your behavior or who you hang out with or your defiance to authority? Search your heart and get rid of whatever is causing the "yard sale" in your temple.

Jesus' anger showed that sometimes anger is an honest emotion with a good reason. Managing your anger and focusing it on something good is what Jesus desires of you.

Understand this, my dear brothers and sisters: you must all be quick to listen, slow to speak and slow to get angry. Human anger does not produce the righteousness God desires.
James 1:19-20 NLT

GOING DEEP ...
Write details of a time when you got angry. Do you regret your actions or words?

Catcher

THE PLAYER THAT IS ALWAYS AT HOME

In 1968, Johnny Bench was the first catcher to ever be named Rookie of the Year. In 1970, he was the youngest player to ever win the National League MVP. He received many other awards during his career and was inducted into the Baseball Hall of Fame in 1989. Interesting fact: he could hold seven baseballs in one hand! He is also known for being one of the first catchers to use a hinged mitt instead of a mitten or pillow mitt which required two hands to catch the ball.

Catchers have equipment that no other position requires:

→ Helmet/mask – protects your head/face
→ Chest protector – covers your chest/ internal organs
→ Shin guards – protects your legs
→ This equipment is designed to protect you from serious injuries.

Would you like to play this position without the necessary equipment? No. That would be crazy! How about when you go to school each day; do you use the equipment that is provided for you? Wait, protection for school? Yes. God gives us all equipment to wear everyday:

→ Helmet of Salvation- believing Jesus died for you
→ Breast plate of Righteousness – being honest/good/fair
→ Belt of Truth – comparing our actions to the Bible
→ Shield of Faith – confident that God keeps promises

→ Sword of the Spirit- our defense is the Word of God
→ Shoes of Peace – a good relationship with God

Just like you would not want to be a catcher without equipment, God does not want you to live your life without His protection. You face so many issues every day that can hurt you. He knows you are not strong enough on your own. Using the gear allows you to catch life's pitches and throw out all the opponents that get in your way. God loves you and desires you to be an amazing catcher in His kingdom.

Put on all of God's armor so that you will be able to stand firm against all strategies of the devil.
Ephesians 6:11 NLT

GOING DEEP ...
Imagine putting on each piece of equipment that God provides. Which do you think it the most difficult to keep on? Which is the easiest? Why?

61

Amy McNeill

Respect

THE DEFINITION OF RESPECT IS A FEELING OF DEEP ADMIRATION FOR SOMEONE DUE TO THEIR ABILITIES, QUALITIES, OR ACHIEVEMENTS.

Among others, Babe Ruth, Willie Mays, Derek Jeter, and Cal Ripken Jr. top some of the MLB lists for most respected players.

Outside of baseball, some people that can earn respect are your parents, teachers, military members, police officers, firemen, the President, athletes, actors, musicians, etc.

On the field, you should respect the umpires, your coaches and your teammates. This is not only the right thing to do, but it also increases your team's morale. When a pitcher is throwing a good game, show him you appreciate his hard work. When a batter lays a sacrifice bunt so you can score from third, give him a "thanks" for doing his job. When your teammate hits a home run, go to home plate and share in his celebration. When a coach spends time teaching you skills, listen and apply it to your game. Feeling appreciated invites everyone to do their best.

One greatly respected person in the Bible is Paul, but he was not always liked. In fact, he was persecuted by many. Paul was visited by Jesus and told to share his story. He went on three missionary trips and started multiple churches using the principles of Christ. Even though he was doing the work of the Lord, his journey was not easy. Paul was beaten, imprisoned, stoned, shipwrecked, and mocked. Through all this, he was persistent to educate people about Jesus. Paul wrote fourteen of the twenty-seven books in the New Testament and some other books were written by people who had communications with Paul. God used

Paul to motivate so many to be committed followers. Generations of people have remarkable respect for Paul's loyalty and boldness.

Above all, show your respect to our Creator. God gives you the ability to play baseball and He deserves your gratitude. Thank God every day for all He has done for you.

Do to others as you would like them to do to you.
Luke 6:31 NLT

GOING DEEP ...

Have you ever felt like someone did not respect you or your opinion? How did that make you feel?

_____

_____

_____

_____

Concessions

HOT DOGS, PEANUTS, CRACKER JACK; DO I HAVE YOUR ATTENTION?

In a single year, there are over 21 million hot dogs sold in MLB stadiums. It is rumored that Babe Ruth once ate 12 hot dogs and drank eight bottles of soda in between a double header. Busch Stadium uses more than 32,000 gallons of nacho cheese in a season. Over 1,000 bags of Cracker Jack are sold during a single game at Fenway Park. Cracker Jack was found in 1893 but did not become a big item until the song "Take Me Out to the Ballgame" was written in 1908.

Concessions are popular at baseball games, but have you ever heard about concessions in the Bible? There are a few examples for us to learn from.

Moses led over a million people out of Egypt. Can you imagine that many people traveling together? They did not know where they were going or how long it would take to get there. They just knew to follow Moses because Moses was following God. So, they found themselves in the middle of the desert with no food.

Miraculously, God provided food. Manna, similar to small pieces of bread, fell from the sky like snow. The people thanked God for not forgetting them.

Another time, a multitude of people followed Jesus to witness the miracles and hear Him speak. As evening came, the disciples suggested the people go home and feed themselves. Jesus had compassion and said He would feed them. A small boy in the crowd had a basket with five loaves of bread and two small fish. Jesus looked to Heaven, gave thanks, and told the disciples to distribute the food. Over 5,000 people were fed fully and leftovers remained.

When you are at a baseball game enjoying your concessions, think about the manna and think about the loaves and fish. Remember that God provides it all. He provided food 4,000 years ago and He provides food for us now. Do not ever doubt His love for you and His promise to supply you with what you need.

And this same God who takes care of me will supply all your needs from His glorious riches, which have been given to us in Christ Jesus.
Philippians 4:19 NLT

GOING DEEP ...

When God provided food from nothing, how do you think the people reacted? Do you give credit to God for providing your food, clothing, and shelter?

Dedication

DEDICATION IS BEING TRULY COMMITTED TO A TASK OR PURPOSE.

The most dedicated player in the MLB was Cal Ripken Jr. Between the years of 1982 and 1998, Cal played in 2,632 consecutive games! No skipped games, no sick absences, no excuses. He showed an example of full out devotion to the game he loved.

Are you dedicated to doing your best in baseball? Do you work on improving your batting? Do you ask for extra practice at your position? How about other areas of your life? You can be devoted to your mom and dad by being obedient. Loyalty is one of the best qualities to have in a good friendship. Focusing on your schoolwork and making good grades shows your dedication as well. Being faithful in your church gives you guidance on how to be truly committed to a purpose.

In the Bible, we see many people who show faithfulness, loyalty, and devotion. One of the most dedicated was a young man named Daniel. He was forced to live in a land that did not worship our God. He was commanded numerous times to stop worshipping God. Daniel could have easily caved to the pressure, been accepted by the people around him, and received no punishment. Instead, he stood firm in his faith and showed the example of full out devotion to the Lord. Even when Daniel faced death by being thrown into the den of hungry lions, he turned to God instead of man. God sent an angel to close the mouths of the lions and cause no harm to His child. When all the people saw this miracle, they understood the God of Daniel was truly worthy of praise. Daniel remained loyal to God no matter the circumstance.

We should strive to be as dedicated as Daniel. When we are loyal and devoted to being faithful, we are examples to others. We can lead others to be a better baseball player, a better student, a better friend, and most of all, a better Christian.

Love the Lord your God with all your heart and with all your soul and with all your strength.
Deuteronomy 6:5 NIV

GOING DEEP ...
Name one thing you have been dedicated to. Was it difficult to remain devoted? Does it make it easier when other people are depending on you?

_____

_____

_____

_____

_____

_____

_____

_____

_____

_____

_____

Stadium Ticket

FENWAY PARK, YANKEE STADIUM, DODGER STADIUM, TURNER FIELD, CAMDEN YARDS, WRIGLEY FIELD

These are a few of the MLB locations you may be familiar with. Each stadium has its own unique style and arrangement. Fenway Park in Boston is the oldest stadium – constructed in 1912. Dodgers Stadium in Los Angeles can hold the most fans – 56,000.

No matter which stadium you plan to attend, you will always need one thing – a ticket. Why is a ticket important? It shows the date, the time, your assigned seat, and the price you paid to attend. With this ticket, you know you own a specific spot for a specific time.

Now, if you were offered the opportunity to go to the most amazing stadium ever, with an amazing view and have unlimited food and drinks, would you want to go? What if I gave you a free ticket? And what if I said you can bring as many friends as you like? Sound good?

Here's your ticket:

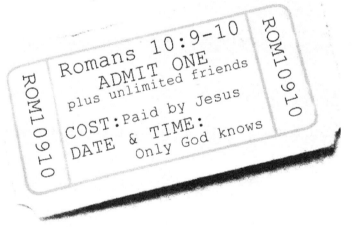

It's really that simple. Jesus has already bought the ticket for you. He is personally inviting you to sit with Him. Heaven is beyond anything you can imagine and it will be worth every step you make to get there. Accept the ticket, make your plans to go, and one day you will enter the most amazing stadium ever!

If you declare with your mouth, "Jesus is Lord," and believe in your heart that God raised him from the dead, you will be saved. For it is with your heart that you believe and are justified, and it is with your mouth that you profess your faith and are saved.
Romans 10:9-10 NIV

GOING DEEP...

List some people you would like to take with you. How are some ways you can inform them?

_____

_____

_____

_____

78

The Game Plan

DO YOU KNOW HOW MANY PEOPLE COACH A MLB TEAM?

Just to name a few... a team manager, a pitching coach, a hitting coach, a first base coach, a third base coach, an athletic trainer. Each is important to the team but only if they work together. To accomplish this, they need a game plan... an established set of guidelines with goals to reach. Then, this plan has to be enforced with the team.

With 162 games in a regular season, a great baseball team doesn't just show up and expect to be good without preparation. They have winter workouts, spring training, practices, and more practices to bring out the best performances in the players.

The coaches evaluate, examine and instruct the athletes on how they can best help the team. Creating and following a plan is essential to the team's success. It is hard work but the players develop a trust for their coaching staff that will hopefully lead them down the winning path.

We are given a great example of a leader in the Bible. God chose a strong young man named Joshua to be the leader of the Israelites after Moses died. On more than one occasion Joshua found himself taking his army into battle. For any other man, this could have been terrifying, but Joshua's plan was to always obey God. He knew God would provide the strength and knowledge needed to defeat the enemy. The people followed Joshua's lead because they knew he was confident in the plan that was prepared. Thanks to God's favor on Joshua's obedience, the army had many victories. Joshua could have easily claimed it was due to his excellent leadership skills, but he did not. He praised God for the plan. He thanked God for showing him the way. He displayed an example of being a leader while also being a servant of God.

Commit to the Lord whatever you do, and He will establish your plans.
Proverbs 16:3 NIV

GOING DEEP …

What is your game plan? Have you asked God to show you the way? Do you want Him to be your leader?

Use the space below to write concerns and goals you have. Commit to a plan that will help you have a winning season for life.

Dear Lord,

I pray that I am the player on the field and off the field that you want me to be. Search my heart and show me how I can serve you better. I want others to see your love through me. Thank you for creating me, teaching me and loving me.

In Jesus' name,

_____

REFERENCES:

New Living Translation
New International Version
New International Reader's Version

MLB.com
Madehow.com
Realclearscience.com
Wikipedia.com
Baseball-almanac.com
Baseballzone.com
Merriam-Webster.com

JOIN THE TEAM ON FACEBOOK

www.facebook.com/catchingjesus

Author email:
catchingjesus@gmail.com

Made in the USA
Monee, IL
04 May 2023

33049217R00052